Neath & Port Talbot
Moments

DAVID ROBERTS

BRYNGOLD

BOOKS

www.bryngoldbooks.com

First published in Great Britain in 2013
by Bryngold Books Ltd.,
100 Brynau Wood, Cimla,
Neath, South Wales SA11 3YQ.

www.bryngoldbooks.com

Typesetting, layout,
editing and design
by Bryngold Books

ISBN 978-1-905900-32-9

Printed and bound
in Wales by
Gomer Press,
Llandysul, Ceredigion.

Contents

A big thank you

Neath & Port Talbot Moments, like all the books in the series before it, is a tribute to those whose support, encouragement in a range of ways, not least the sharing of photographs has made it possible.

Among them are Damien Owen, Laurie Evans, the late Leslie Evans, Raymond Jones, the late Arthur Hendra, Ray Griffiths, Linda & Keith Wathan, Ieuan & Dorothy Jones, the late Bill Young, the late Bill Adams, the late Morris Fish, Sheila Waters, Roger & Veronica Gale, the late John Newman, Brian Harry, Gwyn John, the late Mervyn Roberts, Colin Walters, Tony & Hilary Llewellyn, Raymond Jones, John & Jean Minshall, Lucy King, Eunice Hunter-Rowe, Mrs D Spittle, Margaret Bailey, Janet Jones, Mary Roberts, Lynsey Sly, Elaine Wise, Peter Hitchings, Rhian Lloyd, J Williams, Geoffey Nicholas, Robert Jones, George Evans, Audrey Walters, Keith & Ann Davies, Alan Howell, Ann Brown, Eileen Cottey, Alan Williams, John McArdle, Kay Rees, the late Harry Humphries, Graham and Diane Gilbert, Mike Hopkins, Terry Davies, Enid Farrell, Pamela Parkhill, Pamela Davies, Helen Smith, the late Ken Kingdom, EJ Cross, Janice Austin, John Mathias, Carol Rainford, David Davies, Fred Harris, Margaret & Tony Rowlands, Lindsey Evans, Bob & Ann Merchant, Clive Bowditch, Janet Hussell, Steve & Kay Maclean, John Matthews, Aileen Buckingham, the late Vincent Thomas, Jeff Thomas, Godfrey Eynon, Pamela E Jones, Anita Thomas, Pat Morgan, Graham Haines, Steve Pitman, Peter Stephens, John and Eira Beynon, Steve Dinham, Gareth Bamsey, Allun Davies and Arthur Morris.

Behind the scenes, John Vivian Hughes, Colin Scott, John & Barbara Southard, Neil Melbourne, Rich Brown and Anthony Isaac have all played a vital part in this publication. Finally I must once again salute my wife for her patience, support and committment to the appearance of this and all my other books.

Share your photos

You too, can play a part in recording the history of Neath & Port Talbot by contributing photographs to any possible future pictorial nostalgia books on the towns. Please telephone 01639 643961 or e-mail david.roberts@bryngoldbooks.com to discover the ways in which you can do this. We would be delighted to hear from you. All photographs, black and white or colour, of people, places, events, streets, buildings, schooldays and sport are considered whatever their age, subject or format. They are all promptly returned. Also, if you have missed any of the previous 14 books then contact us now as some titles are still available. You can also check out our website at
www.bryngoldbooks.com
for details of our other fascinating local nostalgia books.

Foreword

It is my privilege as the first citizen of Neath Port Talbot to contribute the foreword to this book as it marks a special milestone for the County Borough. It is the 15th consecutive year that we have been treated to a magnificent photographic album of our towns in days gone by. There are few locations across Britain that can match a record like that.

Those fortunate enough to add Neath & Port Talbot Moments to all the books in the series before it, will have a unique photographic record of the places and faces that have made our proud County Borough what it is today.

All of this is driven by the efforts of the book's compiler, David Roberts, who each year somehow manages to create a fresh and fascinating mix of images that are not only a unique historical record, but one that is so easily accessible and brings much pleasure to many people.

So many people too, have contributed photographs to the books that they have become a vibrant reflection of our community and after 15 years there cannot be many who in one book or another haven't spotted some connection with themselves. Perhaps it is this which makes the book stand out from all the others like it.

While the images are drawn from many sources, it is down to David to create each year's new book and this one like all the rest is an excellent and lasting tribute to his efforts. Neath & Port Talbot Moments is an atmospheric journey back down the years that once again is sure to delight everyone who turns its pages.

**Councillor Marian Lewis,
Mayor of Neath Port Talbot
2013-14**

Moments in time

Neath and Port Talbot are two towns with undeniably separate identities, but for all that they share one common aim — the desire to survive and succeed whatever the world throws at them.

During the 15 consecutive years that this series of books has been appearing, the images they contain have been constantly changing. There is no clearer an indication that the towns themselves have been changing too.

These changes, both large and small, have been necessary to keep pace in an ever-changing world; to meet the pressures and demands that inevitably creates.

Many would agree that more has changed in the lifetime of these books than at any other time in the life of the two towns, but rarely do we stop and take stock of this. So it can occasionally be startling to discover the effects of the race and chase for progress.

Though recent times have brought all-round economic struggle and significant job losses, there remains the optimism that in the future things will once again come good. This, after all is the way it has been in the past.

A reminder of this cycle of life comes with the turning of almost every page in this picture-packed book. So many people have made their own individual contribution of photographs from times past it has once again helped create a unique publication. By sharing their photographs they ensure that we will be able to remember faces, places and events that sooner or later begin to fade in all of our memories. They ensure too that we see our towns and their people from many different viewpoints.

The County Borough of Neath Port Talbot has more than its share of famous personalities, but it is the daily events in the life of its ordinary people that are reflected in the pictures here. This mirror on the past is their own individual way of playing a part in keeping the memory alive.

The good times will return for Neath and Port Talbot. The signs are already there. When they do, generations will sit together, look at this book and marvel at the moments in time it has captured, and the way their towns once were.

**David Roberts
2013.**

About the author

David Roberts has been compiling pictorial nostalgia books for more than 15 years. His publications are widely acknowledged as a valuable contribution to the recording of the way people and places in the area once were.

A long-time journalist and now a publisher, he has strong links with the towns of Neath and Port Talbot, witnessing at first hand many of the events and changes his compelling books depict.

The culmination of his annual picture gathering is always eagerly awaited as people clamour to add to their collection the latest in a series of books that rank as one of the best pictorial social archives in the UK.

This is his 15th book on Neath and Port Talbot, alongside 16 others produced on Swansea where he worked for almost three decades. David, is married, has two grown up children, was brought up in Port Talbot and now lives in Neath.

A member of staff behind the counter of Peacock's stall, Neath Market, 1966. The special offer of the day was nylon stockings for just two shillings and sixpence. That's just over 12p today!

Neath & Port Talbot

Moments

Town times

The Gnoll House and a variety of industrial workings can be seen in the background of this view across Victoria Gardens, early 1900s.

Water Street, Aberavon, presents a tranquil scene around 1900. As the years passed it would become very much busier with traffic.

The Causeway, Aberavon, with its thatched roofed cottages and Capel Moriah just visible in the background, 1890. The photographer certainly seems to have caused quite a stir.

Victoria Gardens Neath, early 1900s. It still remains a green oasis in the centre of the town today.

Looking from The Square towards the tower of St Thomas Parish Church, Neath, early 1900s.

Looking along Station Road in the direction of Bethany Square, 1920s.

The shopping arcade beneath Port Talbot's
Municipal Buildings, late 1950s.

Station Road, Port Talbot, early 1930s. Some of the properties on the left still retained their front gardens at this time.

High Street, Port Talbot, 1957. Clarence Street is in the background.

Windsor Road, looking towards Neath
General railway station, early 1900s.

Parking seems to have been at a premium in Talbot Square, Port Talbot, in 1958.

Green Street, Neath, looking towards The Square, 1910.

Gnoll Walk, Neath, on a sunny winter's day, 1909.

Looking from High Street, Port Talbot, up towards Pentyla, mid-1950s. Aberavon Branch Library is on the left, behind the van.

A fascinating panorama of central Port Talbot, with a smokey steelworks background, mid-1950s.

The Square, Neath, viewed from Green Street, 1910.

Looking down a traffic congested Station Road, towards the railway station, Port Talbot, 1958.

Looking down Water Street towards Port Talbot's Municipal Buildings with the shopping arcade underneath, 1956. The flags may have been to mark the visit to the town of Princess Margaret.

Fresh produce stalls at Neath Market, early 1900s. It was a much more open affair than that which replaced it and exists today.

Aberavon Town railway station, viewed in the direction of Cwmavon, late 1950s.

The Square, Neath, early 1930s. Taking centre stage is the town's first set of traffic lights.

The impressive English Presbyterian Church at the junction of London Road and Greenway Road, early 1950s.

Port Talbot's main police station, Station Road, 1958.

Homes in Castle Street, Aberavon, 1958.

TT Lloyds Store, Neath, 1950. A popular venue for the fashion conscious, this location later became home to the town's Marks & Spencer store.

Heavy traffic on a wet Welsh winter's day in New Street, Neath, mid-1960s.

High Street, Port Talbot, 1958.

Soar Maes yr Haf Chapel, off Windsor Road, Neath,1962 before development of the cattle market site, opposite, the following year when part of its graveyard was taken up by retail development.

Looking out from the open space that was surrounded by the terraced homes of Vivian Square, Port Talbot, 1958. There was only one entrance and exit to this area.

Vivian Square, Aberavon, 1958.

The former entrance to the Bird in Hand field, off Gnoll Park Road, Neath, 1962. The clock tower of St David's Church is just visible on the left.

The Cavendish furniture store, Port Talbot, 1958. It occupied this location at the junction of Church Street and Richard Street for many years.

Early foundation work underway at the Bird in Hand field, Neath, for the town's Civic Centre, 1964.

Neath Hospital Annexe, Wellfield Avenue, mid-1960s. In more recent times it became home to the Gnoll Primary School.

Busy Bethany Square meets Station Road, Port Talbot, 1958.

Orchard Street, Neath, 1966, showing the soon to be demolished Shufflebotham's china store.

A policeman directs traffic at the Water Street and High Street, junction, Port Talbot, 1958. The location was a long-term bottleneck for road users.

The Ivorites Arms, at the junction of Richard Street and Church Street, Port Talbot, 1958.

Neath Castle ruins and alongside, the town's former fire station, 1968.

Looking towards Pentyla and above it Springfield Terrace during the early stages of construction work that saw the M4 slice its way through Port Talbot, early 1960s.

The entrance to the old Town Hall, Neath, viewed from New Street, March 9, 1969.

Some of the stores that once attaracted shoppers to Green Street, Neath, seen in the mid-1960s. This was long before the street was pedestrianised.

Station Road, Port Talbot, at its junction with Bethany Square, 1960. The railway crossing gates are closed forcing traffic to wait for a passing train. This was a bottleneck on the main east-west A48 trunk road, something that wasn't resolved until the opening of the M4, five years later.

Hart Lane leading off James Street, Neath, December, 1972.

Congestion at Water Street, Port Talbot, at its junction with High Street, late 1950s.

Stalls at Aberavon's indoor market, 1960.

Water Street, Neath, January 1977 showing the steel framework for the town's second Tesco building and behind it the magistrates courts.

Looking from Port Talbot's main Post Office, across Station Road, into Grove Place, early 1970s.

The Aberavon Market entrance onto Water Street, 1960.

Bethania Chapel, London Road, Neath, May 1973.

Houses in Duck Street, Neath, 1973.

A Thomas Bros bus heads up Water Street, Port Talbot, 1962.

Demolition of Port Talbot General station, early 1960s.

The sheep pen at Neath abattoir, Eastland Road, 1973.

The road bridge at Bridge Street, over the River Neath that was once the town's main traffic artery on the route to and from the west, March 1973.

A Thomas Bros. bus crosses the High Street bridge over River Afan, Port Talbot, 1962. Such a journey would be impossible today.

Cattle Street, Neath, 1974. Once it was just a narrow thoroughfare. Today it is pedestrianised.

This car park, just off Richard Street, seen in September 1966, served Port Talbot motorists well until it was swallowed up by redevelopment in the years that followed.

The Grand Hotel and opposite, the taxi rank near Port Talbot General railway station, 1967.

Looking out of Neath under the main Swansea to Paddington railway line and along Bridge Street, April 1974.

Looking up Forge Road from Bethany Square, Port Talbot, mid-1960s.

Traffic queues to enter Neath at Bridge Street, April 1974.

Construction work underway on the A465 dual carriageway near the former Neath Riverside railway station, April, 1974.

Shops at Water Street, Port Talbot, 1970, shortly before their demolition to make way for town centre redevelopment.

Preparation work in hand for the building of Neath Magistrates Court, Water Street, 1976.

Water Street, Neath, much of which was demolished to make way for the building of a new Boots the Chemist store and a Tesco store, latterly shared by Tesco and Wilkinsons. Some of the shops demolished were Macarthy's fish and chip shop, Bush Sports and Allin's the grocer. On the opposite side was the Shakespeare pub and the Ancient Briton pub along with the Bird in Hand. The sole survivor is the Greyhound pub seen here in the centre, early 1970s.

High Street, Port Talbot, 1970, prior to the demolition of all the buildings seen here before the birth of the new town centre.

Bethlehem Green Chapel, house and vestry, James Street, Neath, August 1977.

This view, in 1970, from Port Talbot's Municipal Buildings would once have been filled with houses, not cars. The homes vanished during early demolition prior to town centre redevelopment. Until that occurred the area served as a town centre car park.

Looking from Bridge Street, Neath towards Angel Street, on the left, and the Croft, on the right, under the main Swansea to Paddington railway line, 1988. The building in the centre is Great Western Chambers.

Shoppers queue for their bus home in Station Road, Port Talbot, alongside derelict retail properties awaiting demolition, 1970.

Derelict when this picture was taken in 1988, these business premises once thrived at Angel Street, Neath, before town centre redevelopment necessitated their demolition.

Redevelopment of Port Talbot town centre came at a cost as this telling photograph from around 1970 shows. The heart of the old town appeared to have been ripped out.

Looking from Church Place across the flattened rubble that was once the shops and business premises that occupied one side of Water Street, Port Talbot, 1971. The remaining shops would eventually follow suit as clearance work continued.

Early foundation work for the James Street, Neath, retail development, August 12, 1988. The space here was eventually occupied by a Safeway and now Morrison's supermarket.

Lower Water Street, Port Talbot, 1972.

Shops at The Parade, Neath, 1990.

Crowds throng the amusements and rides of Neath's annual fair on the site of the Milland Road car park, September 1997.

A spider's web of timber and steel presented itself to the people of Port Talbot during construction of the town's Princess Royal Theatre, during 1986. It opened the following year.

Demolition of the Civic Centre, Neath, 2008.

Station Road, Port Talbot, Christmas 1993.

Deacons of Jerusalem Chapel, Resolven, sing their praises, 1975.

Neath & Port Talbot

Moments

People power

The Minister of the English Baptist Chapel, Neath Road, Briton Ferry and some of the boys from his congregation, early 1930s.

The vicar of Aberavon, Rev WH Griffiths, with a bible class, outside St Mary's Parish Church, 1902.

A group gathers at Pontrhydyfen in the early 1900s after the killing of a pig. The resulting meat would probably have ended up feeding the family that owned it.

Staff of the newly-opened Lodge Cinema, Briton Ferry on their first annual outing aboard an N & C luxury coach, 1939.

Members of the 2nd (Port Talbot) St Agnes Scout group at Margam Park, Port Talbot, early 1920s.

Connie and George Evans with guests on their wedding day, September 9, 1946, at St Mary's Church, Aberavon.

Wesley Methodist Church, Briton Ferry, was the scene of the marriage of John Melbourne and his bride, Marjorie Rees, on August 1, 1953. They are seen with their guests and the officiating minister.

Young members of Port Talbot Air Training Corps with officers, early 1950s.

Carmel Chapel, Aberavon, was the setting for this wedding line up in 1953.

Members and teachers of the Sunday School at Court Sart Congregational Chapel, Briton Ferry, with their banner, early 1950s.

Members of Herbert Road Baptist Chapel at Walters Road, Melyncrythan, Neath, during their Whitsun procession, 1956.

The Ministers and Sunday School teachers with their pupils at Bethel Methodist Chapel, Water Street, Margam, Port Talbot, 1953. The obedient dog was called Prince.

A group of people gathered outside Baglan Hall, Baglan, mid-1950s.

Male members of the congregation at Herbert Road Baptist Chapel, Melyncrythan, Neath, during their annual Whitsun procession, 1957. They are seen passing the town's St David's Church.

Members of Port Talbot Wheelers cycling club during a Christmas gathering, 1964.

Some of the members of the 10th Port Talbot Scout group at camp with troop leader
Vernon Morgan, early 1960s.

Jim Wise and his bride Elaine Roberts with guests who attended their wedding at St David's Church, Neath, March 21, 1959.

Some of those who helped run the youth club stall at the first bazaar held in the New Vivian Memorial Hall, Port Talbot, 1963.

Three generations, mother Doris, daughter Ann and granddaughter Julie, at Claymill cottages, Baglan, 1961. Behind them construction work is underway on the Baglan dual carriageway.

The gang in front of now demolished houses in Cwmavon Road, near Velindre, Port Talbot, mid-1960s.

Singing star Frankie Vaughan is escorted away from excited crowds at Aberdulais Boys Club during a visit there in the late 1960s. The entertainer was patron of the Boys Clubs' Association. Running alongside is Police Constable Douglas Hitchings.

Easter time in the Children's Ward at Groeswen hospital, Margam, mid-1960s.

Neath singer Allun Davies accompanied by his family gets a civic send off from the town's Mayor Ald R Lloyd Davies and Neath MP Donald Coleman, before leaving to take part in the European Song Contest at Knokke, Belgium, 1968.

Members of Neath Cymrodorion Society, early 1970s.

Girls Brigade members from Wesley Chapel, Taibach, winners of the Urdd Eisteddfod Shield, May 6, 1967. Runners up that year were their colleagues from Trinity Church, Port Talbot.

Staff of the chief executive's department of Afan Borough Council, September 1981 at an event held to mark the retirement of three of its officers, Darwel Thomas, Trevor Hopkins and Jack Lewis. Port Talbot Borough Council had amalgamated with Glyncorrwg Urban District Council in 1974 and became Afan Borough Council.

Members of Resolven Scout group who joined in a village event to commemorate the 50th anniversary of the D-Day landings, 1995.

Members of 8th Neath (Crynant) Cub Scouts at a tramps ball they organised, 1993.

A group of St Joseph's Church parishioners display a banner of welcome for the visit of Pope John Paul II to Wales, 1982.

Well known and much loved Welsh singer and entertainer Ryan Davies addresses the inaugural dinner of Neath Lions Club, at the town's Castle Hotel, 1972.

Members and friends of Port Talbot and District Operatic Society at a social gathering it held in the early 1970s.

Members of the ladies section of Port Talbot East Ward Labour Party with the town's Mayor, Councillor Hilda Mears and her consort, Eileen Owen, outside the Civic Centre, 1990.

Skewen Salvation Army Corps, Young Peoples section, March 1972.

Mayor of Port Talbot, Councillor Hilda Mears and her consort, Eileen Owen, brought a touch of civic pomp to a medieval fayre at the town's St Joseph's Primary School, September 8, 1990.

Members of the youth club at Skewen Salvation Army Corps, March 1972.

Officers and committee members of Resolven Miners Welfare Hall, early 1970s.

Princess Anne, the Princess Royal, meets Port Talbot's leading citizens on the occasion of the official opening of Port Talbot Civic Centre, September 29, 1989.

A cheque for £4,000 raised by a Neath charity group is handed over to the British Diabetic Association to aid their research, March 18, 1982.

Staff of Traethmelyn Primary School, Sandfields, at the Mayor's parlour with Mayor of Port Talbot Councillor Hilda Mears, and her consort Eileen Owen, February 27, 1991.

Viscount Tonypandy and Mr Bryn Thomas with the scrolls they received at a ceremony affording them the Freedom of Port Talbot with dignitaries and guests at a civic ceremony hosted by Mayor of Port Talbot, Councillor Hilda Mears, together with her Consort, Eileen Owen, 1991.

A fundraising event for the Urdd Eisteddfod in Aberafan, 1983.

A gathering of past pupils of Glan Afan School, Port Talbot, at a reunion held at Margam Orangery to mark the school's centenary, 1997.

Foremen at Ford's Jersey Marine plant join together to say farewell to a colleague who was leaving the factory, late 1980s.

Youngsters of the 14th (Neath) Cimla Scout group, including Beavers, Cubs and Scouts, handed over a cheque for £3,000 to the Prince of Wales Committee on July 11, 1989 watched by their leaders, guests and officials of the committee.

A cheque for £1260.57p was handed over in January 2002, as a result of collections made at the Aberafan Shopping Centre to boost the Port Talbot steelworks Blast Appeal.

A group of Neath women who dressed as girls from St Trinian's to collect money for the Cystic Fibrosis charity, 1991.

Port Talbot Amateur Operatic Society's fund raising committee with a delicious looking array of cakes and pastries for sale on a stall they organised at Neath Port Talbot Hospital's fete, 2008.

Excavators claw their way through piles of rubble during the demolition of the bridge that carried the road to Aberavon Beach over the railway at Beach Hill, May, 2006.

Neath & Port Talbot

Moments

Out of town

Sardis Hill, Efail Fach, late 1890s. Worshippers would have needed to be fit to climb its steep hill to reach the now demolished Sardis Chapel, just visible behind the railway embankment.

The view across Glynneath during the 1920s.

There was little traffic to stop these people wandering on the road at Neath Abbey in 1908. It is a far different story today!

Beulah Chapel, also known as the Round Chapel, at Groes Village, Margam, early 1900s.

A very quiet Neath Road, Briton Ferry, 1910.

A locomotive hauls its trainload of empty coal wagons over the viaduct at Pontrhydyfen, which allowed it to continue its journey to Tonmawr and the Afan Valley, 1950s.

Looking up from the Pelenna river towards the main street through Pontrhydyfen, early 1900s.

A solitary horse and cart is the only traffic on the main thoroughfare at Pontrhydyfen on this day in 1910.

Houses and allotments at Oakwood, near Pontrhydyfen, Port Talbot, mid-1930s.

Looking down Villiers Street, Briton Ferry, early 1900s.

Looking down on Efail Fach in the direction of Sardis Hill, with its chapel, 1920.

Baglan Hall in the mid-1930s. It presented an impressive sight complete with its spacious glass conservatory. Sadly nothing remains of the building today.

This building, pictured in the late 1920s, housed Briton Ferry British Legion club for many years. Today, Briton ferry roundabout occupies roughly the same site.

The original wooden pier at Aberavon Beach, 1933.

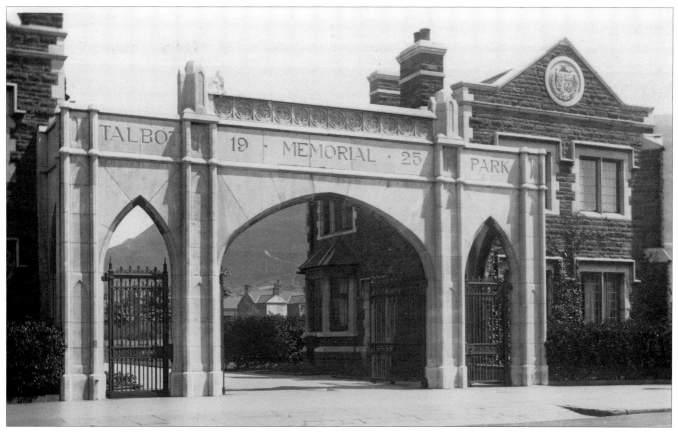

The entrance gates to the Memorial Park, Taibach, Port Talbot, 1935. The park was opened in 1925.

Neath Abbey ruins, 1936.

Sandfields estate, in its infancy, 1952. Lines of prefabs are visible on the left and the much needed housing for incoming workers at the Steel Company of Wales can clearly be seen in various stages of construction.

Construction of Briton Ferry bridge early 1950s. Work started in 1949 and it opened to traffic in the autumn of 1955.

The Evans Bevans brewery at Cadoxton, Neath, early 1950s.

Looking across Velindre, Port Talbot, early 1950s.

The ruins of Baglan House, Baglan, 1950. The former property of the Earls of Jersey, it was built in 1801 and demolished in 1951. Maple Avenue is now built on and around the actual building and much of the greenery and fields in the scene have been covered by further housing development.

Looking at the back of terraced houses at Pantyrheol, Briton Ferry, 1950s.

Drummau Road and Main colliery, Skewen, 1950s.

The river and waterfalls near
Pontneathvaughan turned into a
giant ice sculpture during the severe
winter weather of 1963.

Looking down Crawford Road, Baglan, from Mayberry Road, 1954. The centre of the view is dominated by chimney stacks associated with the heavy industry that provided much employment for the area, including the Albion Steelworks.

Neath Car Sales showroom and petrol filling station, Neath Road, Briton Ferry 1990.

An interesting perspective on part of the sprawling Glannant Estate, Cimla, Neath, mid-1990s.

A Western Welsh bus heads along Commercial Road, Taibach, early-1950s. The Talbot Hotel later became Taibach Rugby Club. The Regent cinema and Taibach Co-operative stores are on the left.

The Glyn Garfield Maternity Unit at Neath General Hospital, 1993. In front of it is the hospital's outpatients unit.

A view from what locals called The look-out, a mountainside rock high above Baglan estate, mid-1950s. Mayberry Road is clearly visible in the centre, with Greenwood Road on the left and Elder Road, still under construction on the right. Ty Isaf playing fields in the foreground have now become the home of Baglan Rugby Club.

The paddling pool complete with its very own lighthouse on Aberavon seafront, 1960. The steel framework of the four winds hotel can be seen in the background.

The basin at Giants Grave on the Neath Canal, 2005.

The promenade, Aberavon Beach, 1962. Miami Beach funfair with its towering Helter Skelter is in the distance and on the left the original beach funfair.

Swan Street and its sub Post Office, Baglan, 1967.

Houses on the Glannant Estate, Cimla after heavy snowfall, 2010.

A view westwards across Velindre, Port Talbot, 1986.

Pupils of Crynallt Junior School, Cimla, dressed in traditional Welsh costume,
St David's Day, 1956.

Neath & Port Talbot

Moments

School report

A Neath Sunday School class, early 1900s.

Pupils of St Joseph's RC School, Aberavon, 1924 with their teacher.

A senior class at Sandfields Secondary School, Port Talbot, 1952.

Class 1C Neath Boys Grammar School, 1948.

Trefelin Infants School, Port Talbot, 1953.

A class at Cwrt Sart Primary School, Briton Ferry, early 1950s.

Class 2C Neath Boys Grammar School, 1949.

Form 2A Dyffryn Grammar School, Port Talbot, 1953.

A class at Gnoll Infants School, Neath, 1953.

Some of the pupils at Dyffryn Grammar School, Port Talbot, together with their teachers and head teacher, 1953.

A group of children at Trefelin Infants School, Port Talbot, 1954.

Pupils of Cimla Infants School with their teacher, 1953.

Pupils of Central Junior School, Port Talbot, 1954.

A class at Cwrt Sart Primary School, Briton Ferry, mid-1950s.

Girls of Gnoll Infants School during St David's Day celebrations, 1956.

Pupils at Cwmafan Junior school with their teacher and headteacher Wyndham Stone, mid 1950s.

A Class at Melincrythan boys Junior School with their teacher, April 1956.

Pupils who attended St Joseph's RC Junior School, Aberavon, 1955.

A class of pupils at Tir Morfa school, Sandfields, with their teacher, 1960.

Cimla Infants School, alongside Cimla Common, Neath, often referred to as 'The Tin School', 1956.

A class at Trefelin School, Port Talbot, 1960.

Neath Girls Grammar School pupils late 1950s.

Cimla Infants School pupils with headteacher Miss Thompson and class teacher Miss Jones during harvest festival late 1950s.

Pupils at Trefelin School, Port Talbot, 1961.

Girls at Alderman Davies' Church in Wales Junior School, Neath, 1965.

A class of pupils at Tir Morfa infants School, Sandfields, Port Talbot, 1965. With them is their teacher Mrs Betty Adams.

Harvest time at Tir Morfa Infants School, Sandfields, Port Talbot, 1970. Mr Bamsey the Headteacher is at the back with staff and the Mayor of Port Talbot, Councillor Edith Letts.

Pupils of Maesyffynon Nursery School, Neath, had a visit from Father Christmas during their Nativity production, 1971.

Staff and pupils from Baglan Junior School with the Mayor of Afan, Councillor Elwyn Williams, in the Mayors Parlour 1980.

Gnoll Infants School pupils, Neath on St David's Day, 1976.

A class at Gnoll Junior
School, Neath, 1975.

Form 5C Dyffryn
Comprehensive School,
Port Talbot, 1980.

Pupils of the Central Nursery
School, Port Talbot all dressed
up for St David's Day, 1977.

Pupils of Crynallt Junior School, Cimla, in traditional Welsh costume, St David's Day, 1980.

Teachers and pupils at Baglan Junior School, 1980s.

Pupils of Melyn Boys Junior School, Neath, all dressed up for their annual Christmas party, 1952.

Neath & Port Talbot

Moments

Special occasions

Residents of Middleton Street, Briton Ferry, during the party they held to celebrate the Coronation of King George V1 in 1937.

A street party in St Catharine's Road, Baglan, 1951 to celebrate the Festival of Britain.

Members of Wern Congregational Chapel, Aberavon, take part in a Whitsun procession, 1952.

Members of Neath Presbyterian Church in Windsor Road during a Whitsun march, early 1950s.

Church and Chapel goers from Aberavon and Port Talbot gather in Vivian Square for their Whitsun meeting after marching through the town, early 1950s.

Members of Neath Mission during the Whitsun procession, 1953.

One of the bands which took part in a Neath Carnival parade marches along Windsor Road, early 1950s.

Residents of Cove Road, Sandfields, Port Talbot, tuck in to the tea party they organised to celebrate the Coronation of Queen Elizabeth II, June 1953.

Members of Orchard Place Baptist Church, Neath during a Whitsun Procession, late 1950s.

Younger members of Holy Cross Church, Taibach, during their Whitsun march, mid-1950s.

Members of Neath Mission during the Whitsun procession, 1952.

A Whitsun procession passes St Theodore's Church hall, Port Talbot, 1956.

Members of Wesley Chapel, Taibach, during a Whitsun procession, mid-1950s.

Friends and relatives celebrate the Golden Wedding of Tom and Margaret Reason of Skewen, Neath, 1956.

Staff of Leslie's store, Green Street, Neath, at their annual Christmas dinner held at the Cambrian Hotel, Windsor Road, December 13, 1961.

Brownies on parade at Aberavon seafront before a civic guard of honour, late 1950s.

Staff of BP Refinery, Llandarcy, Neath at one of the popular dinner dances they held at the Brangwyn Hall in the 1960s.

A group of Port Talbot and Swansea rail workers enjoy a boys night out, 1964.

Members of Salem Chapel Young Wives group after their annual get together at Antolin's
Ros a Mar Rooms, March, 1968.

A religious demonstrator distributes his leaflets outside the Gwyn Hall, Orchard Street, during the
annual procession of witness of Neath Sunday Schools, 1965.

Officers, committee and members of Port Talbot Amateur Operatic Society during a successful get-together, early 1970s.

Participants on one of the floats that took part in a Cimla Carnival, Neath 1974.

Members of the Neath branch of the Liverpool Victoria Insurance Company with some Swansea office colleagues at their annual Christmas dinner and dance in the mid-1970s.

Residents of Wildbrook, Taibach having great fun, during events held there to celebrate the Silver Jubilee of Queen Elizabeth II, July 1977.

Staff of the Town Clerk's department, Port Talbot Borough Council, Christmas, 1972.
The occasion was the Silver Wedding of the Town Clerk, Emrys Griffiths who is seated, centre, with his wife, Barbara.

Employees of the British Aluminium Company's Rheola Works, Resolven, at a function at the plant, mid-1970s.

Residents young and old of Curtis Street, Neath, outside the marquee that housed their celebrations to mark the Silver Jubilee of Queen Elizabeth II, July, 1977.

Marching smartly along Station Road, are these members of the 2nd Port Talbot Boy's Brigade on their way to Trinity Methodist Chapel for a Church parade, 1981.

The Diddymen, one of the prize winning floats in Tonna Carnival, 1977.

Residents of Llewellyn Avenue, Neath, during celebrations to mark the 50th Anniversary of VE Day, May 1995.

Cartoon character Superted was among those present at the opening of a new Principality Building Society office at Commercial Road, Taibach, 1990.

Pupils of Crynallt Infants School, Cimla, dressed up as insects for the Ugly Bug Ball in nearby woodland, 1997.

Some of the participants, dressed as clowns, in the Christmas parade at Port Talbot, 1991.

A lifeguard hoists the red flag for danger at Aberavon Beach as heavy seas
batter the promenade, January 1983.

Neath & Port Talbot
Moments

Working ways

A fascinating view of a heavily industrialised Cwmavon in the early 1900s.

Concrete piles line the ground during foundation work for the construction of the Metal Box Factory, Neath, 1934.

A bird's eye view of the Metal Box factory, Neath, during the latter stages of its construction, 1935.

A group of workmen at Port Talbot steelworks, late 1940s.

The entrance to Briton Ferry Docks, showing Briton Ferry Ironworks, before the building of the Neath River bridge 1950.

Work underway on construction of the Steel Company of Wales, 1950.

Women workers at the Mansel tinplate works, Port Talbot, 1950.

Neath Sheet Steel and Galvanising works, early 1950s.

A colliery at Tonmawr, Port Talbot, 1950s.

The BP oil refinery at Llandarcy, early 1950s.

A group of bus drivers and conductors employed by the Western Welsh bus company alongside one of its vehicles at Neath, early 1950s.

Staff at Cwmafan Junior School, Port Talbot, mid-1950s.

Four staff members of the Western Welsh bus company at Station Square, Neath, take a break between duties. Windsor Road can be seen in the background, mid-1950s.

Tom Ace Rees with two customers, outside his fruiterer's shop, opposite St Agnes Church, Forge Road, Port Talbot, mid-1950s.

Miners with their pit ponies at Graig Ddu Colliery, Tonmawr, Port Talbot, late 1950s.

Staff of the radio and TV department of the Briton Ferry and Neath Co-operative Society's Windsor Road store, mid-1950s. It's site is now occupied by the Neath Jobcentre.

Some of the teachers at
Tywyn Primary School,
Sandfields, Port Talbot, 1965.

Staff and friends from Boots the Chemist, Neath, shortly after the opening of their new premises at
Green Street, seen at a Christmas dinner in the Dragon Hotel, Swansea, where they were joined by
staff from other local Boots stores, early 1960s.

Marion Lillian and Joyce, three employees of the High Duty Alloys company, Briton Ferry, enjoy a tea break, 1964.

Margam wharf, Port Talbot Docks, with blast furnaces dominating the scene, 1960.

Members of the Antolin family with staff at their self service shop, Victoria Road, Port Talbot, 1962.

The EM Edwards works of Wales Gas and alongside it, the Lonlas by-pass, 1968.

Some of the staff of Peacock's clothing stall at Neath Market, 1966.

Aberavon gasworks looking towards the River Afan, 1963.

The Giants Grave Wharf premises of ship-breakers Thos Ward Ltd on the banks of the River Neath at Briton Ferry, 1968.

The DCL Carbide works at Margam, before the building of Kenfig Industrial Estate and the Borg Warner automotive factory, 1964.

The pithead winding gear and baths at Duffryn Rhondda Colliery, Port Talbot, 1964.

The headteacher and staff at Neath Girls' Grammar School, 1971.

Members of the teaching staff at Tir Morfa School, Sandfields, Port Talbot, 1965 - 1970.

Staff at Cefn Saeson Comprehensive School, Cimla, with headteacher Mai Edwards, mid-1970s.

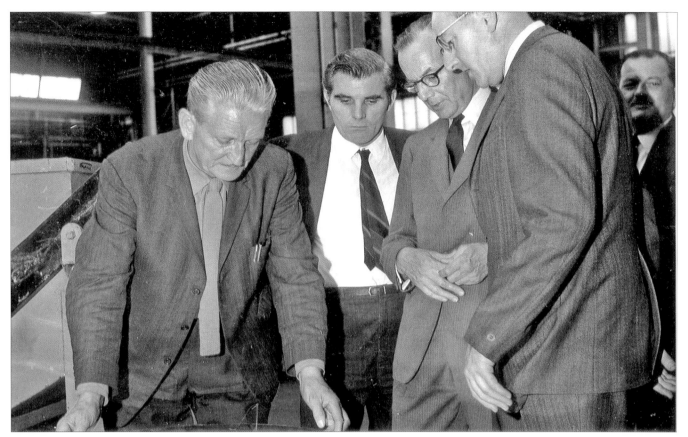

Members of the management team at the British Aluminium Works, Rheola, Resolven, including Mr David Edmunds, 1970s.

Some of the staff of the Port Talbot Borough Council's Town Clerk's department, enjoying a tea break in their canteen, 1972.

David Edmunds, a member of the management team at the British Aluminium Company's Rheola, Resolven plant, examines products at the works with colleagues, mid-1970s.

Members of staff at the Afan Brewery Company, Port Talbot, during a civic visit in 1982.

Employees at one of the blast furnaces at the Abbey Works, Margam, 1980s.

Mark O'Shea pours a pint of beer in his role as the last landlord of the Three Cranes public house, Wind Street, Neath, 1980s.

The BSC Port Talbot works rescue team on top of one of the gasometers at the plant, 1987.

Headteacher Mai Edwards with staff at Cefn Season Comprehensive School, Cimla, Neath, 1981.

This schoolboy will have long grown up by now, but like every motorist, would surely long for the chance to buy fuel at these mid-1970s prices. He was at a Cwmavon, Port Talbot, filling station and believe it or not the price of 5 shillings and 9 pence was per gallon not per litre!

Neath & Port Talbot

Moments

Moving along

The Greek brothers with the cart from which they peddled their wares - mainly rabbits - around the streets of Neath, early 1900s.

A young Baglan brother and sister enjoy an imaginary ride on their father's Triumph motorcycle, 1967.

A Thomas Bros bus awaits its next run from Talbot Square, Port Talbot, to Pontrhydyfen, 1969.

This Napier van was among the earliest commercial motor vehicles seen on the streets of Neath. Operated by Allin's Stores of Wind Street, its driver here in the early 1920s, is George Selby, formerly of Water Street, and later, Tyn-yr-Heol Road, Bryncoch.

An N&C luxury Burlingham Seagull coach leaves its Station Road stop outside Glan Afan School, Port Talbot, mid-1960s.

Driver George Selby at the wheel of Allin's grocery delivery van. The vehicle was a familiar sight around Neath and by the mid-1920s had acquired a windscreen to protect its driver.

Steam ships moored in Briton Ferry Dock, early 1930s.

A tug shepherds an iron ore carrier to her berth at Margam wharf, 1960. Towering over her are the cranes and conveyors that would eventually unload the cargo.

Some of the engineering staff of the Western Welsh bus company's Cadoxton, Neath, depot with one of the vehicles that operated locally, mid-1930s.

A timber carrying vessel unloads a cargo of pit props from Scandanavia at Port Talbot Docks, early 1950s.

A Thomas Bros Leyland Tiger Cub bus at Efail Fach, September 13, 1967. It was heading back to Bethany Square, Port Talbot from Tonmawr.

The 'Dolly' locomotive that carried waste slag to the tip at Briton Ferry steelworks, seen near the end of its life in the early 1950s.

Passengers prepare to board a South Wales Transport double decker in Windsor Road, Neath, late 1950s. The town's Crown Post Office now stands behind the bus.

Bus company, Thomas Bros operated three of these Bristol-make open top double decker buses in the summer months for many years. The braver passengers travelled on the upper deck as in this early 1960s picture of one of the vehicles heading from Aberavon Beach into Port Talbot.

Buses pass in Station Road, Port Talbot near Bethany Square, 1968.

Locomotive 4169 with a local passenger train at Glynneath station, February 2, 1964.

An earthmoving machine involved in clearance work at the bottom of Llewellyn Street, Port Talbot during clearance to make way for the town's multi-storey car park, 1974.

Tank engine No 9475 awaits its next duty at Glynneath locomotive shed on February 6, 1964.

Buses outside the South Wales Transport company's Eastland Road, Neath depot, early 1960s. The depot has long since been demolished and replaced by housing.

This was the car used for many years to transport the Mayor of Port Talbot to civic engagements. On this occasion in 1968 the Mayor, Councillor May Charles was visiting Dyffryn School, Margam, where she is being welcomed by a senior pupil.

Victoria Gardens bus station, Neath, seems to have been the preserve of the Creamline bus company of Tonmawr on this occasion in the late 1970s.

A passenger train leaves Port Talbot Station with Mynydd Dinas in the background, early 1980s.

This loaded tipper truck came to rest against a tree after demolishing the wall of St Michael's Churchyard, Cwmavon, when it careered out of control down Ynysygwas Hill, 1985.

A train of empty oil tankers is hauled up Skewen Bank by a class 60 locomotive on a September evening in 1985. The young lad watching may not have realised that this was an unusual sight as such trains were normally routed along the district line which at the time was closed for repair.

An empty steel train heads down Stormy Bank towards Margam, early 1985.

South Wales Transport buses at the company's Neath Abbey Road, Neath depot April 1982. The building had been inherited from the Western Welsh bus company during re-organisation.

This steam locomotive brought memories flooding back for many people when it operated a series of special runs along the track at the Norbrit Wharf in Briton Ferry in 1985. The runs were organised by the Railway Club of Wales in conjunction with British Rail's Western Region to celebrate 150 years of the founding of the Great Western Railway.

A mixed freight train heads down Stormy Bank towards Margam, 1985.

Three types of transport come together — road, rail and canal. Traversing the other two methods of transport is a class 50 locomotive hauling a Bristol to Swansea train in 1986.

Around 3,000 tonnes of iron ore from Port Talbot Tidal Harbour terminal bound for Llanwern steelworks, Newport, are hauled up to Pyle by two Class 37 locomotives in July 1991.

Children take part in the sack race at a sports day held by Alderman Davies' Church in Wales Primary School, Neath, 1993.

Neath & Port Talbot
Moments

Sporting spirit

Players and officials of Neath AFC, 1906-1907 season.

Aberavon Beach was the scene of a number of car and motorcycle competition events in the 1920s. This one on April 27, 1929 was over a 10 mile course on the sands and was watched by crowds. The Jersey Beach Hotel is in the background and behind it some huge sand dunes.

Skewen Rugby Club during a successful trip to Barnstaple on September 24, 1924, when they beat the home side by 12 points to nil.

Port Talbot Secondary School Cricket squad, 1947 with their teaching coach and right, headteacher Gomer Rees.

Margam United Football team with their trainer, during the 1947- 48 season.

Inside the lounge at Neath Golf Club, 1936.

Port Talbot Secondary School hockey squad, late 1940s.

Neath Rugby Club players and officials, 1928.

Members of the football section of the Employees Welfare Club at Garthmor, Neath, 1933.

The senior rugby squad of Glanafan Grammar School in Trafalgar Square, London, on a trip to Ealing, 1955-56.

Swimmers in the bottom Gnoll Pond, Neath, late 1940s. This was the town's main outdoor swimming pool at the time.

A Glan Afan School cricket team, 1956-57.

Deep in concentration during a Bridge session at Port Talbot YMCA, late 1950s.

Pupils of Alderman Davies' Church in Wales Girls' Junior School, during a gym lesson, 1948.

Glan Afan Grammar School under 14s rugby team, 1963-64 season.

Young members of Neath YMCA gymnastics team proudly show off certificates they received after competition success, 1984.

Briton Ferry Pensioners Bowls Club members during a tour to Great Yarmouth, 1988.

Girls of the rounders squad at Tir Morfa Primary School, Sandfields proudly show off a trophy they won, 1970.

A delighted Arthur Bamsey, of Regent Street East, Briton Ferry with a monster fish he caught off Port Talbot breakwater, 1973. Arthur used a piece of kipper on the end of his rod and line to catch the 27lb 10oz cod.

Tonna AFC football squad. The team were Neath District League winners, 1993.

The junior football team of St Joseph's RC School, Aberavon, 1972. Pictured with teacher Mr O'Brien, the team broke all records for goal scoring and were undefeated.

Members of the Welsh rugby squad during a training session at the Afan Lido in the mid-1970s.

The rugby squad at Tir Morfa School, Sandfields, Port Talbot, 1975.

Swansea City AFC players with youngsters at Aberafan Shopping Centre, 1978.

A Dyffryn School rugby team, Port Talbot, with teachers Les Evans and Alan Huw Thomas, 1975.

Competitors in the Pru Tour Round Britain cycle race which passed through Neath Port Talbot approach Cimla, after the steep climb up Sardis Hill, Efail Fach, September 2004.

Members of local pop group The Questions at the entrance to The Empire ballroom, The Ropewalk, Neath where they performed regularly in the 1960s.

Neath & Port Talbot
Moments

The entertainers

Members of Sandfields Boys School choir, winners of the Royal National Eisteddfod in their class, when it was held at Swansea, 1926.

Female chorus members of a successful amateur operatic production staged at the Gwyn Hall, Neath, late 1940s.

The chorus line of a Melyncrythan Amateur Operatic Society production, 1961.

Popular female vocalist Gay Sheridan performing with her band in a Neath venue, mid-1960s.

Neath singer Allun Davies in Knokke, Belgium as a member of the team representing GB at the Knokke European song contest, 1968. He is pictured with team mates Friday Brown and Marty Wilde.

The choir of St Paul's Church, Aberavon, mid-1960s.

Women and a young boy who were members of a fund raising group that staged a concert for the British Red Cross at Margam Orangery, late 1970s.

Skewen Salvation Army Corps band, March 1972.

Members of the male chorus in Port Talbot Amateur Operatic Society's production of
The Merry Widow, 1975.

Skewen Salvation Army Corps Songster Brigade, March 1972.

The back stage crew of Neath Amateur Operatic Society's production of Oliver enjoy a moment of relaxation and joviality, 1974.

Pupils of Central Infants School, Port Talbot during a concert, 1982.

A scene from Robert and Elizabeth staged by Neath Amateur Operatic Society at the Gwyn Hall, Neath, during November 1990.

Members of Port Talbot and district Amateur Operatic Society's Youth Theatre group, late 1990s.

Rehearsal time for some of the young members of Port Talbot Amateur Operatic Society's theatre group concentrating hard with their choreographer and accompanist, 2007.

Members of Neath Amateur Operatic Society in the town's Windsor Road on a float advertising their 1992 show, George M - Yankee Doodle Dandy, during Neath Carnival.

Visit www.bryngoldbooks.com for other titles available including:

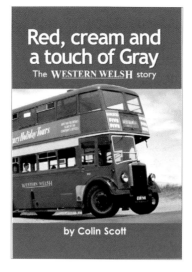

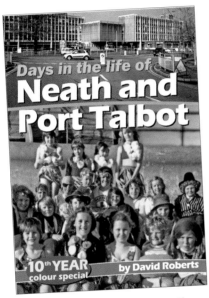

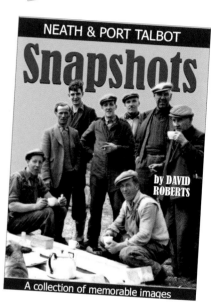

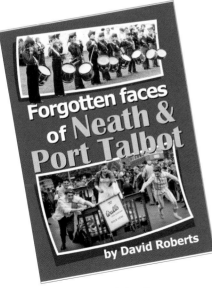

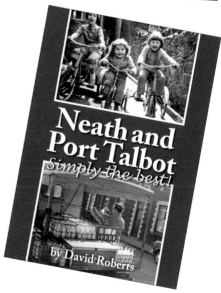

To buy any of these titles tel: 01639 643961
email: info@bryngoldbooks.com or visit
www.bryngoldbooks.com